A CHILDREN'S PLAY

The Magic Flute

MOZART'S FAMOUS OPERA IN PLAY FORM

DRAMATIZED BY JUNE WALKER ROGERS

THE DRAMATIC PUBLISHING COMPANY

THE MAGIC FLUTE
A Straight Play Version
For Five Men and Six Women
plus nine roles that can be played by either; extras as desired
(Doubling possible)

C H A R A C T E R S

TAMINO . . . . *a prince*
THE DRAGON
MIRANDA
CASSANDRA . . . .*followers of the Queen of the Night*
MELISANDRA
PAPAGENO . . . .*a birdcatcher*
QUEEN OF THE NIGHT
FIRST SPIRIT
SECOND SPIRIT . . . . *guides*
THIRD SPIRIT
FIRST SERVANT . . . . *at Sarastro's Temple*
SECOND SERVANT
PAMINA . . . . *a princess*
MONOSTATOS . . . . *guard at the Temple*
OLD MAN . . . . *Keeper of the Temple*
SARASTRO . . . . *High Priest of the Temple*
FIRST ELDER
SECOND ELDER . . . . *Wise Men of the Temple*
THIRD ELDER
PAPAGENA . . . .*a young girl*

ANIMALS, SARASTRO'S FOLLOWERS, SYMBOLS OF FIRE AND WATER, VARIOUS OFFSTAGE VOICES.

THE MAGIC FLUTE may be done as a straight one-act play, with or without the Mozart music. Some of the Mozart arias may be included at the discretion of the director.

3

CHART OF STAGE POSITIONS

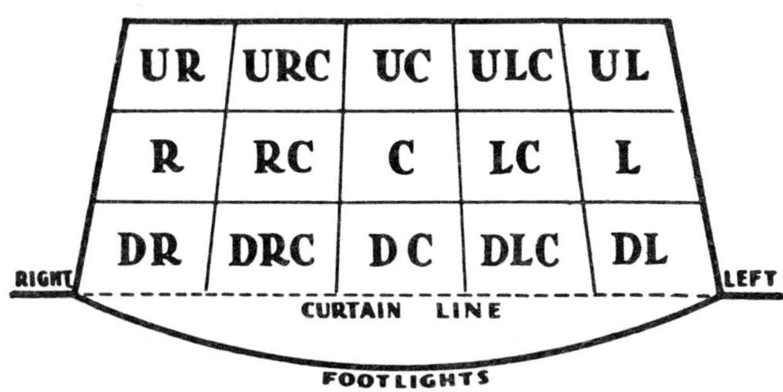

STAGE POSITIONS

Upstage means away from the footlights, *down-stage* means toward the footlights, and *right* and *left* are used with reference to the actor as he faces the audience. R means *right*, L means *left*, U means *up*, D means *down*, C means *center*, and these abbreviations are used in combination, as: U R for *up right*, R C for *right center*, D L C for *down left center*, etc. A territory designated on the stage refers to a general area, rather than to a given point.

NOTE: Before starting rehearsals, chalk off your stage or rehearsal space as indicated above in the *Chart of Stage Positions*. Then teach your actors the meanings and positions of these fundamental terms of stage movement by having them walk from one position to another until they are familiar with them. The use of these abbreviated terms in directing the play saves time, speeds up rehearsals, and reduces the amount of explanation the director has to give to his actors.

4

SCENE: A wood. This can be as simple or elaborate as you wish. The only necessary scenery is a large rock DL and a cave UC. UC, in the cave, is an opening masked by drapes.)

AT RISE OF CURTAIN: Sounds of running can be heard off L, and weird menacing monster sounds. After a beat, PRINCE TAMINO, a handsome young man, runs on DL. He is frightened. He pauses, looks back off L.)

TAMINO. It's getting closer. (He runs off DR.)

(The DRAGON enters DL, pursuing Tamino, lets out his weird dragon cry and chases after Tamino, exiting DR. TAMINO runs on again R, looking a little more tired. He grabs at the belt around his waist.)

TAMINO. My dagger! I've lost my dagger.

(There is another dragon cry from R and TAMINO runs off L. The DRAGON enters R, looks around, cries and follows Tamino off L. TAMINO re-enters UL, running downstage, staggering now.)

TAMINO. I haven't the strength to go any
        further! Help! Someone! Please help me!
        (He collapses, hitting his head on the rock
        DL.)

(The DRAGON enters UL, pursuing him, sees
        him unconscious on the ground, approaches
        him slowly, is about to attack, when three
        ladies — MIRANDA, CASSANDRA and
        MELISANDRA — run on from R, each with
        a silver spear poised for attack.)

MIRANDA (the first lady, lunging at the DRAGON
        and wounding him; he falls back near the
        proscenium). Die, monster! Die!
CASSANDRA (the second lady, circling around
        the fallen dragon). Death to all evil.
MELISANDRA (the third lady, as all three plunge
        their spears into the dragon). Finished!
        It's finished!
MIRANDA (nudging the dragon with her foot).
        We must be sure.
CASSANDRA (reassuring her). Miranda, nothing
        could survive that. (She points to the spear.)
        Our mighty silver spears have never failed
        us, now have they?
MELISANDRA (shining the tip of her spear with
        her hand). Never.
MIRANDA (moving to TAMINO). And now let
        us see what we have won. My, my! This is

a handsome prize!

CASSANDRA (excited). Yes, isn't he?

MELISANDRA. The Queen must be told!

CASSANDRA (pushing MELISANDRA). Right.
    And I'd hurry if I were you, Melisandra.

MELISANDRA (resisting). One more push like
    that, Cassandra, and you'll end up like that
    dragon over there.

MIRANDA (stepping between them). Please!
    Please. Both of you go and I will stand
    guard over this — this — (With melting
    tones.) — gorgeous creature.

CASSANDRA (facing MIRANDA). Oh, yes, you
    would, wouldn't you? Well, get that out of
    your mind. I wouldn't trust you alone with
    him for one minute. (There is a clap of
    thunder offstage and the three freeze,
    listening.)

MIRANDA. She's angry. Our Queen is angry.

CASSANDRA (shaking). We've been stupid . . .
    letting a mere mortal interfere with our duty.

MELISANDRA. Yes. So the only solution is
    that we must all return to the Queen and
    bring her back here.

CASSANDRA. She's sure to forgive us when she
    sees what we have saved for her. Isn't she?

MIRANDA (nodding). Wouldn't you, if you were
    she? I know I would. (Looks at TAMINO
    closely again.) Oh! He's beautiful. If I
    could only run my fingers through his hair
    once. (Starts to touch his hair when there
    is another clap of thunder.)

CASSANDRA (shouting off stage). We're coming!
    (Then, in a loud whisper to MIRANDA.)
    You're weak! Just close your eyes and keep
    walking, and the temptation will be over.
    (Exits into cave.)
MIRANDA (weakly). I know . . . I know I'm
    weak . . . (Closes her eyes, holds out her
    hand to MELISANDRA.)
MELISANDRA (as she leads MIRANDA out).
    There, there, you poor dear. We'll stand by
    you and lead you back on the right track.
    Stop trembling! I've never seen you like
    this.
MIRANDA (as they exit into cave). I've never
    been like this. (Opens her eyes and looks
    back at TAMINO.) Do you think I could
    have a lock of his hair? (MELISANDRA
    pulls her off into the cave.)

(There is a sound of bird calls and PAPAGENO
    enters R. He looks as though he is half
    man, half bird. On his back is a cage filled
    with birds.)

PAPAGENO (using his bird-call whistle). Come
    out! Come out! Papageno is here! (Blows
    whistle again.) Join your fine feathered
    friends. . . . twit-tweet — twit-tweet.
TAMINO (stirring, opening his eyes, hearing the
    bird calls). Birds. I must be in heaven.
    (Sits up, sees PAPAGENO.) I've never seen
    a bird like that! (Whistles toward

PAPAGENO.) Hello there . . . whatever you
are.

PAPAGENO (startled). I didn't see you! Where
were you hiding?

TAMINO. A talking bird. A parrot. You're the
biggest parrot I've ever seen.

PAPAGENO. I'm not.

TAMINO. Yes, you are! I've never seen a six-
foot parrot.

PAPAGENO. I'm not a parrot at all. You're
trying to trick me. (Accusing.) You're
from the Queen of the Night! She's always
spying on me.

TAMINO (standing). I don't know any Queen of
the Night. But why would anyone spy on
you? You look perfectly harmless. Strange,
but harmless.

PAPAGENO. Strange? Strange, you say? Why?
Because of these feathers?

TAMINO (thinking it over). I guess that is why.

PAPAGENO. How else can a bird catcher catch
his birds? (He takes the cage from his back,
shows it to TAMINO.) They think I'm one
of them. (To the birds in the cage.) Coo . . .
coo . . . . . coo . . .

TAMINO. But you're not?

PAPAGENO. No.

TAMINO. You're sure?

PAPAGENO. Yes.

TAMINO (testing). Would you like a worm?

PAPAGENO (insulted). Certainly not!

TAMINO. What do you do with all of them,

after you've caught them?

PAPAGENO. I give them to the Queen of the
        Night in exchange for bread and wine. It's
        a happy arrangement.

TAMINO. Not for the birds.

PAPAGENO. How dare you question me? I've
        never seen you before. It's rude to question
        strangers. Who are you and what are you
        doing here?

TAMINO. I'm Prince Tamino and I was separated
        from my group when the Dragon attacked us.
        (Sees the Dragon.) The dragon! What a job
        you did on him. You saved my life.

PAPAGENO (who had hidden behind TAMINO
        the moment the Dragon was mentioned,
        looking out now, frightened, shaking). I
        saved your life?

TAMINO. Of course, my friend. Don't be
        modest. Who else could have killed it?

PAPAGENO. Killed? (Comes from behind
        TAMINO cautiously.) That's right. Who
        else? (Goes nearer Dragon.) It does look
        dead. . . . Of course, with dragons, can
        you ever be sure?

TAMINO. I'm sure. He's dead.

PAPAGENO (straightening up, sticking out his
        chest). Well . . . I must admit . . . it was
        extraordinarily brave of me.

TAMINO. And without any weapons? How did
        you do it?

PAPAGENO (bragging now). Well, I . . . I just
        went up to him — (He swaggers, illustrating.)

— and I looked him in the eye — (He thrusts
out his face with a mean look.) — then I
grabbed him by the neck — (He grabs his
own neck.) — and I wrestled and wrestled
— (He rocks from side to side, illustrating.
Gasping now.) — till I brought him to his
knees . . . (He falls to his knees.) And with
sheer brute strength I squeezed the life out
of him.

(MIRANDA, CASSANDRA and MELISANDRA
    enter from the cave.)

MIRANDA, CASSANDRA and MELISANDRA
    (shouting). Papageno! (Frightened, he falls
    forward on his face.)
CASSANDRA. Papageno!
PAPAGENO (rising). Oh, you wonderful ladies
    . . . . thank you . . . you saved me from
    destruction . . . at my own hands.
MIRANDA. Fool!
PAPAGENO (modestly). Sometimes I don't
    know my own strength.
MELISANDRA. The birds!
PAPAGENO (picking up the cage and handing it
    to her). The Queen must be anxious for
    these.
MELISANDRA (sarcastic). You brave, brave
    hunter.
PAPAGENO (holding out his hand). My payment,
    please.
MIRANDA (giving him a jug). A jug of water.

PAPAGENO. Water? (Tastes from the jug, spits
     it out.) Water! I can wash in the pond.
     (Hands jug back to MIRANDA.) You must
     be joking. And where is my loaf? I'm
     hungry.
CASSANDRA (giving him a rock). Try eating
     this.
PAPAGENO. A rock? (Beginning to be nervous,
     ingratiating himself.) I'm sure it's delicious,
     but . . . I'm having a little trouble with my
     teeth. (Hands the rock back.) I'd prefer
     to go back to our usual arrangement. Wine
     and bread? (They say nothing.) What's
     the matter? Are you angry with me?
     (MELISANDRA takes a padlock attached
     to a rope from her pocket and ties it around
     Papageno's head so the padlock covers his
     mouth.)
MELISANDRA. You're an idiot, Papageno, and
     must be punished for telling lies.
TAMINO. I don't know what he could have done
     to offend you, but I must speak. He saved
     my life.
MIRANDA (softening). Oh, the beautiful one's
     awake.
CASSANDRA. And he's as compassionate as he
     is good-looking.
MELISANDRA. You must be told the truth,
     Prince Tamino.
TAMINO. You know my name?
CASSANDRA. The Queen of the Night, our
     royal sovereign, knows all. And tells us.

We . . . we killed the dragon. (Pointing to
the padlock.) And this . . . this is the
Queen's punishment for Papageno's taking
credit for deeds done by others. For shame,
Papageno.
PAPAGENO (unable to speak, but trying).
Mmm . . . mm . . . mmm . . .
TAMINO (putting an arm around PAPAGENO).
Forgive him, my lovely saviors. (The ladies
react to the flattery.) It was my fault for
assuming, and no real harm was done, now,
was it?
PAPAGENO (pleading). Hm . . . mm . . .
yaummm . . .
MIRANDA. He must pay a penalty. I think the
Queen was more than kind. Only a padlock.
I could have come up with something much
more imaginative. Then you'd never do it
again, Papageno.
PAPAGENO (moving away from her). Grr . . .
ourw . . . grr . . .
MELISANDRA. But, Prince Tamino, we have
something for you.
TAMINO. No padlock, I hope.
MELISANDRA (giving him a locket). No. A
precious gift. Compliments of the Queen.
A portrait of her daughter.
TAMINO (looking at it). I'm overwhelmed.
MIRANDA. The Queen was counting on that.
CASSANDRA. Do you find the portrait pleasing?
TAMINO. An understatement. Never have I
seen such beauty. I must meet her.

(There is a clap of thunder and the QUEEN
    OF THE NIGHT appears in the cave.)

QUEEN (moving to TAMINO). I knew you were
    to be the chosen one. (Touches his hand.)
    Why are you trembling? Surely you can't
    be afraid of me? The Queen of the Night?
    Did I not send my ladies to kill the dragon?
TAMINO (bowing). And for that, I'm deeply
    grateful. Always.
QUEEN. Always?
TAMINO. Always.
QUEEN. And you find my daughter desirable?
TAMINO (looking at locket). More than any girl
    I've ever seen.
QUEEN. Enough to rescue her from the tyrant
    who has imprisoned her?
TAMINO. Enough to go through hell and high
    water.
QUEEN (knowingly). That, too. (PAPAGENO
    shakes his head "no" to warn TAMINO.
    MELISANDRA pokes him, and, frightened,
    he stops.)
TAMINO. And the tyrant? Do I know him?
QUEEN.   His name is Sarastro.
MIRANDA, CASSANDRA and MELISANDRA
    (hissing like cats). Ssssss . . . arassssssssstro.
PAPAGENO (falling to his knees in fear).
    Mmmmmmmmmmmmmm.
CASSANDRA. Off your knees, bird brain!
    Sarastro can't use his magic on you while
    we're here.

TAMINO. Magic? Is this Sarastro a magician?
    (The QUEEN extends her arm upward and
    there is a clap of thunder.)
QUEEN. Nothing to compare to me! (Points
    to TAMINO.) You must kill Sarastro!
MIRANDA, CASSANDRA and MELISANDRA.
    Kill! Kill! Kill!
TAMINO. Kill? I hadn't thought of anything
    that violent.
QUEEN. How can you have qualms about
    someone so evil? Kill Sarastro and my
    daughter Pamina will be your bride.
TAMINO (looking at locket again). Pamina . . .
    Pamina . . . what a lovely name. A name
    to match that lovely face. Pamina . . . my
    bride to be.
QUEEN (clapping her hands). Then you'll do it?
TAMINO (reluctantly, nodding). If there's no
    other way. . . .
MIRANDA (twirling around TAMINO). No other
    way!
CASSANDRA and MELISANDRA (also twirling
    around him). Sarastro will die! Sarastro
    will die!
QUEEN (stopping them with a gesture). There
    will be plenty of time for celebrating . . .
    later. We must let our Prince begin his
    journey. (She takes a silver flute from her
    pocket.) This flute will keep you free from
    danger. It has great magical power.
TAMINO (accepting it). A magic flute?
QUEEN. Its music can accomplish anything good

that you wish. Never lose it, and it will
prove to be the best friend you've ever had.
Nothing . . . absolutely nothing . . . will be
impossible.

TAMINO. Just holding it seems to give me a
sense of strength I never knew I had.

QUEEN. The next time I see you will be the
happiest day of my life. My daughter will
be home and Sarastro will be dead.

MIRANDA, CASSANDRA and MELISANDRA.
Dead! Dead! Dead! (The QUEEN holds
her arms high in the air; there is a clap of
thunder and she exits into the cave.)

PAPAGENO (pointing to padlock). Hmmm . . .
mm . . . mmm? (The three ladies whisper
among themselves. MIRANDA exits into the
cave. The other two circle and taunt
PAPAGENO.)

CASSANDRA. Maybe we should boil him in oil.

MELISANDRA. I think not. My pet snake would
love a playmate. Let him come with me.

(PAPAGENO runs and hides behind TAMINO.
MIRANDA returns from the cave.)

MIRANDA. The Queen is merciful. She wants
the padlock removed.

CASSANDRA (taking it off). And I had such
great plans for this feathery friend. . . .

MIRANDA. Papageno, you may now speak but
if you ever tell a falsehood again, your fate
will be decided by Melisandra and Cassandra.

(The two ladies hiss at him like cats.)
PAPAGENO. I will never lie again. (Bowing.)
     I am your obedient servant.
MIRANDA. Good. Then you will heed the
     Queen's wish that you accompany Prince
     Tamino.
PAPAGENO (backing up). But that's dangerous!
CASSANDRA. Then you're mine . . .
PAPAGENO. That's dangerous-er. (Jumping to
     Tamino's side.) What are we waiting for?
     Let's go kill Sarastro.
MIRANDA (taking a pouch from her shoulder
     and putting it around Papageno's shoulder).
     And for further protection, in that pouch
     there is a set of silver bells. They will guide
     you to safety, Papageno. (There is a clap of
     thunder.)
MELISANDRA. We must return to the Queen.
     (Starts toward cave.)
TAMINO. But who will show me the way to
     Sarastro's temple?
MIRANDA (as the ladies go into the cave). Three
     young spirits will soon appear and they will
     lead you. Fear not, handsome prince, all
     will end well.
PAPAGENO (nudging TAMINO). I get the feeling
     she likes you.
TAMINO (dismissing the thought). Oh, Papageno . . .
PAPAGENO. If only the day would come when
     some girl would want me. Oh, yes, I'd gladly
     moult all my feathers for the right girl. You
     may not believe this, but I get lonely. (From

different sides of the stage, there is an echo
of the word: "Lonely . . . lonely . . .
lonely . . ." PAPAGENO looks both ways
for the source of the echo.) And when
you're lonely your imagination plays strange
tricks. (Echo says "Tricks . . . tricks . . .
tricks . . . ")

(The three SPIRITS enter from three different
areas.)

FIRST SPIRIT. We are here . . .
SECOND SPIRIT. To guide you . . .
THIRD SPIRIT (bowing). Follow us. (The
SPIRITS dance around TAMINO and
PAPAGENO as they lead them off stage R.)

(Two SERVANTS enter stage L, pushing on a
small flat on wheels that depicts a formal
garden. They place it DL, downstage of
the Dragon, which now exits behind it.
As they enter, the FIRST SERVANT is
laughing.)

FIRST SERVANT. It's the funniest sight I've
ever seen.
SECOND SERVANT (nervous). Shh! Shh!
FIRST SERVANT. I can't help it. It's too
funny . . . just thinking of Monostatos
chasing after poor Pamina. . . .
SECOND SERVANT. It won't be so funny if
he hears you.

FIRST SERVANT. He's such a clumsy oaf. . . .
    (Imitating him.) Oh, Pamina . . . Pamina
    . . . be mine . . .
SECOND SERVANT (becoming PAMINA). Oh,
    Monostatos . . . you clumsy oaf . . . (He
    starts off L giggling.)
FIRST SERVANT (following, pretending to be
    Monostatos). Stand still, Pamina . . . be
    mine!
SECOND SERVANT. You'll have to catch me
    first . . . (They run off L, laughing.)

(PAMINA, a lovely girl, runs on DL, fearfully
    looking over her shoulder.)

PAMINA. Please. Please leave me alone.

(MONOSTATOS, a smiling menace, enters DL.)

MONOSTATOS. Pamina, I mean you no harm.
    Can't you see what my feelings are for you?
    (He advances toward her.)
PAMINA. Evil! You're evil, Monostatos!
    Sarastro will have your head if I tell him
    about your actions.
MONOSTATOS (laughing). He'd never take your
    word against mine.
PAMINA. You're supposed to be guarding me
    . . . but I fear you more than any other
    harm that could come to me.
MONOSTATOS (taking her arm). I deserve to
    have you for my bride. Sarastro owes me

    that.
PAMINA (struggling). I'd rather be dead.

(PAPAGENO enters R, backing on stage, looking
    off.)

PAPAGENO. Where did everyone go? (He turns
    and sees PAMINA.) My goodness! What a
    beauty! (MONOSTATOS makes a growling,
    angry noise and PAPAGENO turns to face
    him. Each is frightened at the sight of the
    other.)
PAPAGENO and MONOSTATOS. The devil!
    It's the devil! (They run off in opposite
    directions.)
PAMINA (looking after both). How bizarre.

(PAPAGENO runs back on, looking over his
    shoulder, as though pursued. He bumps
    into PAMINA.)

PAPAGENO. Excuse me! I'm in a hurry! (He
    stops, realizing it's PAMINA, turns and looks
    at her closely.) Pamina. You must be
    Pamina, the daughter of the Queen of the
    Night.
PAMINA. I am. How did you know that?
PAPAGENO. You look like the portrait she
    gave to Prince Tamino when she ordered
    him to come and free you. (Pulls her hand.)
    Follow me!
PAMINA (pulling back). How do I know that I

can trust you? That you're not another one
of Sarastro's guards like Monostatos? (Nods
in the direction he went off.)

PAPAGENO. Monostatos? Do you think I
could ever be a friend of that thing? Ugly!
He's ugly! I imagined he was the devil.

PAMINA. You're not far wrong. (Takes his
hand.) Please forgive me, but I can see now
that you are a good man, a loving man.

PAPAGENO (sadly). Loving . . . how true! But
unloved in return. I have neither wife nor
sweetheart. Would you believe that all this
manliness is going to waste?

PAMINA (reassuring him). Someday your dream
girl will appear and you will never be lonely
again.

PAPAGENO (sighing). That's what all the girls
tell me. Then they go off with somebody
else. When she finally appears, I hope I
won't be too old to appreciate her. It took
one second for Tamino to know that you
were the only one for him.

PAMINA (pleased). Tamino loves me. (Confused.)
Have I met him?

PAPAGENO. No. He fell in love with your
portrait . . . and as far as he was concerned,
that was it. One, two, three. (Snaps his
fingers.) Some people have all the luck.

PAMINA (laughing). But love should be a two-
way arrangement. I haven't fallen in love
with his portrait yet.

PAPAGENO. Oh, you would! But why don't we

save time? Come with me. I'll show you the real thing. We've wasted too much time already. After I get you and him together, I've got to find a girl for me. (He takes her off R.)

(The SERVANTS return L and take the garden flat off. At the same time the three SPIRITS enter from upstage, move to the cave and turn the set around. The opposite side is painted to represent a temple with a practical door at C. Over this door is a sign bearing the word "Wisdom." There is a door painted on each of the side panels. When the SPIRITS have the temple in place, TAMINO enters.)

FIRST SPIRIT. This is as far as we can go.
SECOND SPIRIT. One of these doors holds a key to your future.
TAMINO. Can you tell me if I will rescue Pamina?
THIRD SPIRIT. Patience! Patience!
FIRST SPIRIT. We do not have the power to offer you any further help, but we know that if you are brave you will find your happiness. Farewell! (Exits L.)
SECOND SPIRIT (following first). Farewell! Remember, one of those doors must open.
THIRD SPIRIT. Find the right one. Farewell. (He also exits L. They are gone.)
TAMINO (going to door R). This door looks

like the one I should enter. (Knocks on door.)
VOICE BEHIND DOOR. Stand back! Stand back!
TAMINO (backing away). I guess not. (Goes to
    door L.) Maybe this is the one.
VOICE BEHIND DOOR. Stand back! Stand back!
TAMINO (backing away and moving to door C).
    There's no other choice, so . . .

(TAMINO lifts his hand to knock, and the door
    is opened by an OLD MAN.)

OLD MAN. Are you searching for something,
    young man?
TAMINO. For the key to my happiness.
OLD MAN (coming downstage). How can you
    find happiness when you come here with
    vengeance in your heart?
TAMINO. Vengeance toward a tyrant who does
    not deserve your protection.
OLD MAN. There is no tyrant here.
TAMINO. Is this not the land of Sarastro?
OLD MAN (nodding). He is the high Priest of
    Wisdom. (TAMINO moves to enter the
    door.) But wait! For your own good, you
    must tell me why you feel this hatred for
    him? What has Sarastro done to you?
TAMINO. It's what he has done to the Queen of
    the Night . . . abducting her daughter.
    Never have I seen such an unhappy woman.
OLD MAN. You must not believe everything
    she tells you. She is a vindictive woman.
    She is using you for her own ends.

TAMINO. Do you deny that Sarastro has Pamina?
OLD MAN (re-entering the Temple). I am bound
    by an oath of secrecy. I can tell you no more.
TAMINO. Please, please . . . Can you tell me if
    Pamina is still alive? I must know. Is
    Pamina alive?
VOICES INSIDE TEMPLE (chanting). Pamina
    lives! Pamina lives!
TAMINO (shouting). Thank you! Thank you!
    I will be able to endure anything now that I
    know she is alive. (Takes out the flute and
    begins to play.) Pamina! Can you hear my
    music? The music that is in my heart? It
    is for you! (As he plays, ANIMALS — lions,
    tigers, one, few or several — come from the
    woods and dance. He stops playing.) The
    music is magical . . . but not, alas, magical
    enough to make Pamina appear. (From off-
    stage comes the sound of Papageno's bells.)
    Papageno's bells! (He plays the flute in
    answer.) Maybe Pamina is with Papageno.
    Keep playing, Papageno. The bells will
    lead me to you. (The bells stop.) Now why
    did he stop? (Plays flute, then listens.) I'll
    find you! I must find you! (He exits UR,
    playing the flute, the ANIMALS following
    him.)

(PAMINA enters DR.)

PAMINA. I'm sure the flute sounds were coming
    from this direction. Papageno!

(PAPAGENO enters DR, tiptoeing, finger over
     his mouth to silence her.)

PAMINA. What's the matter? Why are you
     suddenly so quiet?
PAPAGENO. Shh! We're being followed.

(MONOSTATOS jumps out from DR.)

MONOSTATOS. Not followed. Stalked!
     You've been stalked and I'm ready for the
     kill! Aaaa-eeeee!
PAPAGENO (holding the bells high). Stand back!
     (As MONOSTATOS advances, PAPAGENO
     thrusts the bells in front of him and shakes
     them in fear.) Don't come a step closer
     or . . .
MONOSTATOS. Or? (As bells get louder, his
     expression softens and a silly grin comes
     over his face.) Or I will pirouette the night
     away. . . . Wheeeee. . . . (He pirouettes
     around and off the stage, giggling.)
PAMINA (touching the bells). We should all
     own such magical bells. What a marvelous
     way to rid ourselves of our enemies.
PAPAGENO (bragging). Well, the bells did have
     something to do with it, but personally, I
     think that monster realized he was up against
     a bigger, stronger, braver man! (A trumpet
     sounds inside the temple. PAPAGENO
     freezes at once, shaking in fright.)
VOICE IN THE TEMPLE. Long live Sarastro!

Hail to Sarastro!

(PAPAGENO begins to run but is stopped as
     SARASTRO and his FOLLOWERS come
     from the Temple. Seeing him, PAPAGENO
     hides behind PAMINA.)

PAPAGENO (peeking around PAMINA at
     SARASTRO). Oh, my! What can we
     possibly tell Sarastro?
PAMINA. The truth! (Kneeling before
     SARASTRO.) I beg for your understanding,
     my lord. I am guilty . . . guilty of running
     away from that evil monster Monostatos.
     He is not to be trusted. He frightens me.
SARASTRO (tenderly). Rise, Pamina. I want
     you to be happy. You know that.
PAMINA (rising). Now. If you did, you'd let
     me go back to my mother, not keep me a
     prisoner.
SARASTRO (shaking his head "no"). You must
     never see your mother again. She is a bad
     influence and will use any means, including
     you, to destroy me and my teachings.
PAMINA. She loves me.
SARASTRO. She loves power more.

(MONOSTATOS enters, dragging TAMINO on.)

MONOSTATOS. Stop struggling! (Pushes
     TAMINO toward SARASTRO.) Kneel
     before your master!

SARASTRO. That will not be necessary.
TAMINO (seeing PAMINA). It is she!
PAMINA. It is he! (To PAPAGENO.) That is
    Tamino, isn't it?
MONOSTATOS. Sarastro, do not be fooled by
    her seeming innocence. She and the prisoner
    have plotted against you. He must be
    punished.
PAMINA (rushing to embrace TAMINO). No.
    No! You must not harm him!
MONOSTATOS (pulling them apart). Now you
    can see with your own eyes who is your
    loyal subject. Sarastro, I want my reward.
SARASTRO. And you will get what you deserve.
    For all the deceitful things you have done
    behind my back, under the guise of devotion,
    you will be taken away and given seventy
    lashes. (Sarastro's FOLLOWERS grab
    MONOSTATOS.)
MONOSTATOS (roaring). I will return! There
    will be revenge! (He is pulled offstage.)
PAPAGENO (making sure Monostatos is out of
    earshot). You can't threaten us, you big
    bully! (Turning back to the others.) He's
    getting what he deserves.
SARASTRO (holding up his hand). Enough.
    Papageno, go into the Temple and wait for
    your next instructions.
PAPAGENO (apprehensive). I thought I was
    finished with this whole business. Tamino
    has found Pamina and I'm ready to go home.
SARASTRO (pointing). To the Temple, Papageno,

before we cut off a few of your fancy
feathers. (PAPAGENO runs obediently into
the Temple. PAMINA grips Tamino's hand.)
Fear not, Pamina.

PAMINA (bravely). I fear nothing when I'm holding
Tamino's hand.

SARASTRO. That is a good sign. I am sure your
love will endure the tests of time. But for
the moment you are to be separated.

TAMINO. Separated? We've only just met!

SARASTRO. Pamina is coming with me and you
will join Papageno in the Temple. The Elders
are waiting for you there.

TAMINO (sending PAMINA off). It's all right.
I am willing to do anything to make you
mine and you must have faith in me. I
know now that Sarastro would never harm
you. (He waves to PAMINA as she exits
with SARASTRO.)

(TAMINO goes toward the Temple. The
set divides, moving apart to reveal
PAPAGENO, sitting, surrounded by
the ELDERS.)

PAPAGENO. Tamino! What a relief to see you!

TAMINO (to ELDERS). I am here. Now, what
do you want of us?

FIRST ELDER. The important question is, what
do you want?

TAMINO. I want the right to claim my love.

SECOND ELDER. Would you be willing to die

for her?
TAMINO. I would.
PAPAGENO. Die for love? Tamino, think again.
THIRD ELDER. Papageno, you are not prepared
      for the same sacrifice?
PAPAGENO (shaking head "no"). All I ask of
      life is good food, a nice home and a loving
      wife. But if I sacrifice my life to get it, then
      what have I got?
FIRST ELDER. If you follow our laws and pass
      our tests, you will have a pretty wife who
      will be everything you could ever imagine.
PAPAGENO. You have anyone special in mind?
FIRST ELDER. Her name is Papagena.
PAPAGENO. Papagena? What a pretty name!
TAMINO. Papageno-Papagena . . . She sounds
      perfect.
PAPAGENO (dubious). I admit it sounds good —
      (To ELDERS.) — and it's not that I don't
      trust you, but could I see her first?
SECOND ELDER. You will see her in due time.
      But you cannot speak to her until permission
      is granted. And you, Tamino, must undergo
      the same test of silence with Pamina or any
      other woman who comes into your presence.
      You must not speak a word.
TAMINO. That seems easy enough.
THIRD ELDER. We will leave you now.
      Remember the rule of silence! (The
      ELDERS exit and the lights dim.)
PAPAGENO (calling after them). Did you have
      to turn the lights off just 'cause you left?

(To TAMINO.) I don't like the dark.
TAMINO. Patience, Papageno. This may be part
    of the test.

(Suddenly, MIRANDA, CASSANDRA and
    MELISANDRA appear, glowingly lit, in
    three different areas upstage. The effect
    is eerie.)

MIRANDA. You are in danger!
MELISANDRA. You must escape!
CASSANDRA. Go now or you are doomed!
MIRANDA. Doomed!
MELISANDRA. Doomed!
PAPAGENO (whispering). Tamino, let's get out
    of here.
TAMINO. Shh! We can't! We're committed!
MIRANDA. Our Queen is waiting. You know
    you're one of her favorites, don't you,
    Papageno? (She comes closer to him.)
PAPAGENO. Ah . . .
MELISANDRA (teasing). We've missed you more
    than we can say, Papageno. (PAPAGENO
    opens his mouth to answer. TAMINO
    claps his hand over Papageno's mouth.)
TAMINO. Don't answer, Papageno. You must
    not break your oath.
CASSANDRA. Have you no tongue of your own,
    Papageno? Speak to me.
TAMINO (to PAPAGENO). Be still! (There is
    the sound of thunder and the beating of a
    gong.)

(The three ELDERS appear and drag the three
    ladies off.)

MIRANDA, CASSANDRA and MELISANDRA
    (screaming at PAPAGENO and TAMINO).
    Fools! You are fools!
PAPAGENO (quivering). You know they're
    right? I do feel like a fool. What am I
    doing here? Who needs this? All I wanted
    was a bride.

(An OLD HAG hobbles on from L.)

HAG (cackling). Bride? You looking for a
    bride? How about me? (PAPAGENO makes
    a disgusted face.) Don't be so picky. Look
    around! I'm the only volunteer.
TAMINO. Where did she come from? I'm going
    to get one of the elders. This could be
    another trick of the Queen's. (Starts off
    after Elders.) Remember! Don't speak!
    (He exits.)
HAG (cuddling up to PAPAGENO). Alone at
    last. I thought he'd never go. (She cackles.
    He turns away.)
PAPAGENO (to himself). I wish he'd stayed.
HAG. Isn't that sweet. You want a witness to
    our betrothal. Heh heh heh. You may hold
    my hand. (She holds it out to him; then,
    coyly:) But you mustn't try to kiss me!
    (She holds her face up to his.)
PAPAGENO (forgetting the oath, repulsed). Kiss

you! Don't worry. You're safe with me!
HAG. Oh, Papageno, how honorable of you.
    You want to wait until we're married.
PAPAGENO (moving away from her). Married!
    You're too old to get married. Even if you
    were younger.
HAG. Married, indeed! Indeed! Indeed! Heh
    heh heh. Otherwise, my plumed peacock,
    you'll be imprisoned forever. And if you
    think I'm ugly, you should see dungeon food.
    Well, need I say more?
PAPAGENO. Imprisoned! Dungeon food!
    (Thinking it over and rushing to the hag.)
    Take my hand!
HAG (coyly). But do you really love me?
PAPAGENO (holding out one hand, covering his
    eyes with the other). Can't you tell? (HAG
    turns her back to audience, then removes
    false nose and wig.)
HAG. Heh heh heh. At my age it's difficult to
    be sure of anything. Oh, to be young again!
PAPAGENO (still covering his eyes). You!
    Young! Can you remember that far back?
    (HAG steps out of the hag's cape, revealing
    herself as an attractive girl dressed in a
    feathered skirt resembling Papageno's
    feathered costume.)
HAG (smiling). I'll be forever young, Papageno,
    with you by my side.
PAPAGENO (slowly peeking through his fingers
    at her). You . . . you . . . (Dropping his
    hand, overjoyed.) Papagena! Papagena!

(He rushes toward her.)

(The SECOND ELDER appears.)

SECOND ELDER. Stop! (PAPAGENO freezes
        in position.) You are not worthy of her
        yet. Go, Papagena.
PAPAGENA (disappointed). Oh! Oh, well!
        (She waves to PAPAGENO and, with a
        wiggle of her feathers, exits.)
PAPAGENO. That's not fair!
SECOND ELDER. Good things in life should
        not come easily or they are not appreciated.
PAPAGENO. Oh, I appreciate. Believe me, I
        appreciate. That Papagena! Whoooooo . . .
        (He flutters his feathers.)

(TAMINO enters, followed by the three SPIRITS.)

TAMINO. I hope I got back in time.
PAPAGENO. You missed meeting my Papagena.
TAMINO. You broke your oath of silence.
SECOND ELDER. He does not have your
        strength of character, Tamino.
PAPAGENO. So? You knew that from the
        beginning. I should get a couple of points
        for trying.
SECOND ELDER (laughing). Maybe, Papageno.
        I'll bring that up at the next Elders' meeting.
        In the meantime, stay strong, Tamino. (He
        exits.)
FIRST SPIRIT (giving the magic flute to

TAMINO). We are returning the Magic Flute
   to you. Never put it down again.
TAMINO. I didn't know I had. I won't again,
   I promise. (FIRST SPIRIT exits.)
THIRD SPIRIT (giving the bells to PAPAGENO).
   And here are the bells, Papageno.
PAPAGENO. Those aren't my bells. I've got my
   bells. (He looks, sees he doesn't have them.)
   Oh! When did you take them?
THIRD SPIRIT. You dropped them . . . on the
   path . . . carelessly. . . .
PAPAGENO. I wasn't careless. . . . (Taking bells.)
   A little sloppy, but not careless. (THIRD
   SPIRIT exits.)
SECOND SPIRIT. Use these gifts with discretion
   and you will be blessed. (SECOND SPIRIT
   exits.)
PAPAGENO (playing bells). You think the bells
   could bless us with a little food?

(THIRD SPIRIT returns with a bowl of fruit.)

THIRD SPIRIT (handing bowl to PAPAGENO).
   For your delight. (THIRD SPIRIT exits.)
TAMINO (playing the flute). The sight of Pamina
   would be feast enough for me.

(TAMINO continues playing and PAMINA enters.)

PAMINA (rushing to TAMINO). The flute is
   loud and clear. I have been waiting for
   your signal to join you. (TAMINO keeps

playing, avoids looking at her.) Aren't you
glad to see me, Tamino? Papageno, what's
the matter with him?
PAPAGENO (gobbling fruit). Tamino, the fruit
is sweeter than any I have ever tasted. Try
some. (Offers bowl to TAMINO, who shakes
his head "no.")
PAMINA (pleading). Tamino, I cannot believe
you would be rude to me.
PAPAGENO (holding up a piece of fruit).
A pomegranate! I never thought I'd see
a pomegranate. What luxury!
PAMINA. Tamino, if this is your way of re-
jecting me, then I wish you would say so.
(TAMINO tries to comfort her with his eyes
but she does not understand.) How cruel
life is! I thought I had found the meaning
of love but if you do not feel the way I do,
then there is nothing left for me. (She waits
for him to answer but there is no reply. She
turns to PAPAGENO, who has been watching
her. He immediately begins to eat an apple.)
I feel humiliated! (She begins to cry, starts
off. TAMINO stops playing the flute and
takes a step toward PAMINA. She turns
toward him, but to avoid her eyes, he turns
away again and plays the flute. PAMINA
runs off.)
PAPAGENO. I don't know how you could keep
your silence. And not even eat!
TAMINO. It is the most difficult thing I have
ever done in my life. I hope I won't regret it.

PAPAGENO. She looked completely lost.
TAMINO. Papageno, stop it! Sarastro said I
        must pass these tests and I must have faith
        that he will be a man of his word and that
        this will end with Pamina and me together.
PAPAGENO (his hand on Tamino's shoulder).
        You're a better man than I, Tamino. Your
        love is stronger, your faith is stronger, and
        you must be hungrier.

(The trumpets sound and the FIRST ELDER
        enters.)

FIRST ELDER. Sarastro is waiting. Follow me!
        (PAPAGENO and TAMINO follow the FIRST
        ELDER upstage and exit. The two halves
        of the Temple come together again.)

(PAMINA enters downstage, weeping.)

PAMINA. Nothing! I have nothing! I am
        nothing!

(PAMINA sits on the rock and covers her face
        with her hands, weeping. MONOSTATOS
        enters, sees her, creeps up behind her,
        touches her shoulder. Thinking it is
        Tamino, she touches his hand.)

PAMINA. Oh, my Prince! (She rises, turns,
        sees MONOSTATOS.) Monostatos! Ugh!
MONOSTATOS. Don't draw back from me.

(The QUEEN OF THE NIGHT enters in a rage,
     pushing past MONOSTATOS, and goes to
     PAMINA.)

QUEEN. Ungrateful daughter! I had everything
     so well planned and now Sarastro has gotten
     to Tamino. He is a lost soul. Now, only
     you can save us. (She pulls a dagger from
     her robe.) You must take this dagger and
     kill Sarastro!
PAMINA (holding the dagger as though it were
     red hot). Kill? Murder? Mother, I cannot
     kill.
QUEEN. If I am to rule again, you must! Do
     not try to see me again until you have
     succeeded. (She exits.)
PAMINA. I cannot murder . . . not even for my
     mother.
MONOSTATOS. Give the dagger to me and show
     that you trust me. I know a way to save you
     and your mother. The dagger, please. (He
     holds out his hand and PAMINA reluctantly
     gives him the dagger. Then he grabs her by
     the wrist.) Now, you must love me!

(SARASTRO enters unnoticed.)

PAMINA. No!
MONOSTATOS. No? Then you will die! (He
     raises the dagger and SARASTRO, behind
     him, grabs his raised arm.) Sarastro! I am
     innocent! It is not what it appears!

SARASTRO. You are never what you appear.
      Go!
MONOSTATOS (threatening). The Queen of the
      Night will welcome me. Your days are
      numbered. (He exits.)
PAMINA. Please don't punish my mother. She
      has not been the same since I was taken
      from her.
SARASTRO. I know everything, my child. And
      within these walls, revenge is unknown. We
      try to guide with friendship and instill
      brotherly love.
PAMINA. I have loved but I have lost.
SARASTRO. No. Tamino is faithful to you and
      loves you alone.
PAMINA. Then why did he turn from me? Why
      did he remain silent?
SARASTRO. He was forbidden to speak. He
      loves you enough to defy death for you.
PAMINA. I should never have doubted him. It
      was weak of me.
SARASTRO. Love must endure many trials.
      Come. Tamino waits for you.

(SARASTRO claps his hands and the SPIRITS
      appear carrying a veil.)

SARASTRO. You must be prepared for the
      meeting. (The SPIRITS put the veil over
      Pamina's face.)

(PAPAGENO runs on. He stares at the veiled girl.)

PAPAGENO. Papagena? Are you Papagena?
    (PAMINA shakes her head "no.") Then why
    are you hiding your face? Sarastro, how can
    you be so cruel to me?
SARASTRO. Papageno, when you learn patience,
    your life will fall into place. (All but
    PAPAGENO exit, leaving him bewildered.)
PAPAGENO. As soon as I come, everybody goes.
    Where can she be? (Calls.) Papagena!
    Papagena! Lovely, sweet Papagena! (He
    whistles a bird call.) Coo . . . coo . . .
    Won't you answer me? If only I hadn't
    seen her, I wouldn't have known what I
    have lost. Now, I can never forget her.
    (Calls.) Papagena! Did you hear that? I'll
    never forget you. The pain in my heart is
    unbearable. (Shouts.) I must die to end
    this pain. (He takes some rope from his
    pocket.) I have a rope. I'll make a noose.
    Hanging is the only way to go! (He listens.)
    Is there no one around to show some com-
    passion for a lovesick fool? (He listens again.)
    I'll give you one more chance to make me
    change my mind. Once I tie the noose,
    there'll be no stopping me. (He hears
    nothing, shrugs, begins to make the noose.)
    If there's anyone who cares, you don't have
    much time. Papageno, no one cares. Put
    the noose around your neck. (He puts the
    noose around his neck.) World . . . good-
    bye! Before I leave, I'll count to three . . .
    (Considers.) Ten. . . . No, three. One . . .

two . . . two and a half . . . two and three
quarters . . . (Listens one final time and
hears nothing.) That did it. It's farewell.
Three!

(The three SPIRITS rush on.)

FIRST SPIRIT. No, Papageno!
PAPAGENO (relieved). Oh there you are!
SECOND SPIRIT. Stop!
THIRD SPIRIT (grabbing rope away from him).
     Take that silly noose off.
PAPAGENO. You took a long time coming.
THIRD SPIRIT. We did not believe you would
     lose the love of living so easily. Everyone
     should know you live only once and each
     moment should be cherished.
PAPAGENO. That sounds good. And I used to
     believe it. But nothing seems to work out
     for me any more.
SECOND SPIRIT. Then take your silver bells
     and let them play.
PAPAGENO. The silver bells! I forgot all about
     them. (Takes out bells.) A little sound here,
     a little sound there! Carry your tune to the
     ears of my sweetheart.

(The SPIRITS dance off to the tune of the bells,
     returning immediately, holding PAPAGENA
     by the hand.)

PAPAGENO. Papagena!

PAPAGENA. Keep playing, dear Papageno. This
    is a joyous moment. (The SPIRITS and
    PAPAGENA dance around him once, then
    the SPIRITS exit, leaving them alone.)
PAPAGENO. Are you to be mine forever?
PAPAGENA. Forever.
PAPAGENO. The elders have looked down on
    me with favor.
PAPAGENA. They know you are a good man,
    Papageno. A little foolish, perhaps, but a
    good man.
PAPAGENO. We must find Tamino and share
    our happiness with him. (There is a clap of
    thunder which frightens them and they hide
    to the side of the Temple.)

(MONOSTATOS enters, followed by the QUEEN
    OF THE NIGHT and her three LADIES.)

MONOSTATOS. We are near the Temple.
QUEEN. Be still. If we are to succeed we must
    surprise them.
MIRANDA (hissing). Surprise!
CASSANDRA and MELISANDRA. Attack!
    Attack!
MONOSTATOS. But I must know you will keep
    your word. Your daughter must be mine.
QUEEN. She shall be yours in return for your
    faithfulness, o cunning Monostatos.
MIRANDA. Cunning Monostatos. (A sound of
    thunder.)
MONOSTATOS. Quiet. That sound is ominous.

CASSANDRA. And it's drawing nearer.
QUEEN. We must fear nothing now. We are so
        close to Sarastro's total destruction. Listen
        to nothing but the hatred in your heart.
        (The thunder gets louder and louder and
        there is a flash and then total darkness.)

(When the lights come up, MONOSTATOS, the
        QUEEN OF THE NIGHT and the three
        LADIES have vanished.)

PAPAGENA (peering out). They have vanished.
PAPAGENO (coming out). The earth just
        swallowed them up.
PAPAGENA. A fitting end for evil. (Putting her
        arms around him.) And a beginning for us.
PAPAGENO. If only Tamino is still alive . . .
        and well enough to care. The bells will lead
        us to him if he is. (He plays the bells, and
        he and PAPAGENA exit R.)

(A fiery light appears stage L and the FIRST and
        SECOND ELDERS appear, standing over
        the light with arms extended.)

FIRST ELDER. Man while following his path in
        life must go through trials of fire and water,
        temptation and hell.
SECOND ELDER. His character will develop,
        and his moral strength. Nothing will seem
        impossible.

(The ELDERS step aside, revealing TAMINO behind
     them.)

TAMINO. I have no fear. I know my path now.
PAMINA (calling from offstage). Tamino! Wait!
TAMINO (startled). Was that Pamina?
FIRST ELDER. Yes. Sarastro is bringing her
     here.
TAMINO. I must know. Am I released from my
     oath of silence? If not, I don't think I would
     want to see her again before my next trials.
SECOND ELDER. Silence is no longer required.
     Rejoice!

(SARASTRO enters, holding PAMINA by the
     hand.)

SARASTRO. Your moment to be remembered,
     Pamina.
PAMINA (bowing to TAMINO). Tamino, my
     Prince!
TAMINO. My lovely Pamina.
PAMINA. I will never leave your side again.
SARASTRO (questioning her). With complete
     trust?
PAMINA (lifting her veil). I trust my love.
TAMINO. I can ask no more. (Holds out his
     hand.)
SARASTRO (fading into the background with
     the ELDERS). The gates unfold for you!
     (Thunder. The lights flicker on and off.)

Your destiny is up to you.

(From every side, figures in red leotards enter,
      representing FIRE. They form a block
      around PAMINA and TAMINO.)

TAMINO. The flames are strong . . . the heat
      intense.
PAMINA (putting her hand on his shoulder). Take
      your magic flute and play. Its music will
      protect us on our way.
TAMINO (looking at flute). How can we be sure
      of that?
PAMINA. My father with all of his great magical
      powers made that flute from the branch of
      an old oak tree. The tree is still standing,
      stronger and more beautiful than ever.
      (TAMINO puts the flute to his lips and as
      the music is heard, the flames part and make
      a clear path for him and PAMINA.)
OFFSTAGE VOICES (from all sides). First fire
      . . . now water . . . do not be afraid!

(The red-covered figures back off and exit.
      Figures with blue and green streamers
      attached to their arms and around their
      waists representing waves of WATER,
      float on downstage with their arms extended
      and block the path of PAMINA and TAMINO.)

TAMINO. The water is even more forbidding.
      The waves are surrounding us . . . how can

we escape?
PAMINA. The flute, Tamino. . . . Play the flute.
    (The music is heard again and the waves
    make a path for PAMINA and TAMINO,
    then exit.)
TAMINO (embracing PAMINA). We have come
    through fire and water unharmed.
PAMINA. The magic flute has been our faithful
    friend.

(A gong sounds, and SARASTRO and the ELDERS
    enter from upstage.)

SARASTRO. We rejoice! You have attained
    your goal! Victory is yours!
ELDERS. The good have conquered.
TAMINO. I had much magical help from my
    sturdy flute.
SARASTRO. Tamino, the flute is but a symbol.
    You and your Pamina have the strength of
    character to overcome life's obstacles.
    Nothing else is needed.
TAMINO (putting the flute in his pocket). That
    may be, but I must admit, having the flute
    was very comforting.

(The SPIRITS enter downstage, dancing, scattering
    flower petals. They are followed by
    PAPAGENO and PAPAGENA.)

TAMINO. Papageno! How good to see you.
    And with Papagena! We have both achieved

our heart's desire.
PAPAGENO (holding Papagena's hand). The
      spirits have been kind to me, and understanding.
SARASTRO (putting his hand on Papageno's
      shoulder). Sometimes the weak need a little
      more compassion to help them through the
      rough spots. (Putting his other hand on
      Tamino's shoulder.) You and Tamino have
      shown us that youth can have the wisdom
      and faith to overcome destructive forces . . .
      that you can work for a future full of beauty
      and fulfillment.
PAPAGENO (reminding him). And Papagena!
SARASTRO (amused). And Papagena. We know
      that you and your children and your children's
      children will continue to value the ideals that
      make the world a better place in which to
      live.
TAMINO. We have worked and struggled and
      dared to make this so.
SARASTRO. There is no other way. (He smiles
      at them. The couples embrace.)

CURTAIN

Very little scenery and few properties are required to present this play. Place and time are evoked by appealing to the imaginations of the spectators.

PROPERTIES

GENERAL:
   Cave formation, with masked opening in center, which reverses to a temple with door (practical) in center. Sign over door: WISDOM. The center door is flanked by two painted doors. Large rock.
   Small flat (formal garden) on wheels.

TAMINO: Belt around waist, silver flute given him by the Queen of the Night.
MIRANDA: Silver spear, jug of water, pouch containing silver bells.
CASSANDRA: Silver spear, rock.
MELISANDRA: Silver spear, padlock attached to rope, locket.
PAPAGENO: Cage filled with birds, bird-call whistle, rope.
QUEEN OF THE NIGHT: Silver flute, dagger.
FIRST SPIRIT: Tamino's flute, flower petals.
SECOND SPIRIT: Veil, flower petals.
THIRD SPIRIT: Papageno's bells, bowl of fruit, flower petals.
FIRST SERVANT ⎤
SECOND SERVANT ⎦ : The small garden flat on wheels.

PAPAGENA: False nose and wig, long cape over
   feathered skirt.

COSTUMES

Costumes should suggest a more or less traditional
fairy-tale style: long skirts for the ladies, tunics
and tights for the men.

Papageno wears a short feathered cape, perhaps a
feathered cap. Papagena dresses in a similar fashion,
with a feathered skirt or dress. On her first
appearance she wears an ugly false nose and a
haggish wig, and her feathered costume is con-
cealed by a long, full cape.

The spirits and elders may wear long, flowing
gowns, the spirits ethereal and the elders more
somber.

The dragon and the animals may be costumed as
simply or as elaborately as desired. An eared cap,
mittens, tail and foot coverings of the appropriate
color would be sufficient for each animal. A
complete costume would of course further enhance
the play, but is not necessary for a successful
presentation.

The symbols for Fire wear red leotards and tights.
The symbols for Water wear blue and/or green
leotards and tights, and have blue and green
streamers attached to their arms and waists.